Stand Up To Sexting

AN OPEN CONVERSATION FOR PARENTS & KIDS

BUSHEL
& PECK
BOOKS

Text copyright © 2020 by Christy Monson and Heather Boynton
Illustrations copyright © 2020 by Albert Pinilla

Published by Bushel & Peck Books
www.bushelandpeckbooks.com.

Bushel & Peck Books is dedicated to fighting illiteracy all over the
world. For every book we sell, we donate one to a child in need—
book for book. To nominate a school or organization to receive free
books, please visit www.bushelandpeckbooks.com.

LCCN: 2019956094
ISBN: 9781733633574

First Edition

Printed in China

10 9 8 7 6 5 4 3 2 1

Stand Up To Sexting

AN OPEN CONVERSATION FOR PARENTS & KIDS

Christy Monson, LMFT
Heather Boynton,
Professor of Child Development

Contents

Welcome! This book is meant to facilitate meaningful conversations between you and your children. Let's get you talking!

INTRODUCTION

Wait, So You Really Wrote a Book About Sexting?

Absolutely! And if you have kids or work with kids, you probably aren't all that surprised. According to a recent survey[1], parents now rank sexting among their top-ten parenting concerns—and even higher than smoking, teen pregnancy, or school violence. When we told one parent what we were writing, she said, "YES! I've been wanting to talk to my daughter about that, but it's just so hard to talk about. I need this book." If that sounds familiar to you, welcome! Whether you're a parent, teacher, grandparent, faith leader, or mentor, you're in good company.

The Problem with Sexting

Some say that sexting is just innocent sexual exploration by teens. Normal adolescent stuff, right? Unfortunately, wrong. Sexting is fraught with emotional, mental, social, and even legal consequences. Consider these:

- Sexting is linked with anxiety, depression, and even teen suicide[2].
- Sexting reduces securit and commitment and increases conflict in relationships[3].
- Sexting triggers the same addiction-forming release of dopamine as other addictions like drugs and pornography[4].
- Sexting can be illegal and, depending on the state, bring criminal charges of child pornography.
- Sexting has become a new form of cyberbullying and even blackmail.
- Sexting can begin as early twelve years old, according to recent estimates.[5]

Why We Need to Talk About It with Our Kids

S imple: because no one is. Thanks to school programs and government initiatives, kids are well-versed in the perils of drugs and alcohol. But sexting? It's the elephant in the room that everyone—especially parents—are uncomfortable talking about. But it's precisely us parents and those who work with kids who need to take the lead on such an important topic.

That's why we wrote *Stand Up to Sexting*.

KNOWLEDGE IS POWER!

How to Use This Book

The book is meant to facilitate meaningful conversations between you and your children. The goal is to get you talking! Each mini chapter addresses a specific topic and comes with five sections:

- **TEACH**: Each chapter begins with a few simple expert guidelines about the chapter's topic.

- **STORY**: To help kids put themselves in real-life scenarios, each chapter includes a story where the problems, solutions, and consequences of sexting are explored in a real-world setting.

- **CONVERSATION**: Several Q&A prompts follow the story to help parents and kids begin a meaningful conversation about what just happened in the story, what could have gone differently, and what a child should know going forward.

- **WRITE**: Writing helps children form their own thoughts and opinions. Each writing section comes with a few prompts to help jumpstart a child's critical thinking.

- **GOAL**: After learning and discussing, the final step is acting. In each chapter, we invite kids to set a personal goal for what they will do in their own lives to stay safe from sexting.

DO YOU HAVE TO READ THE WHOLE BOOK AT ONCE?

No! In fact, the content is broken down into twelve miniature chapters. You can pick and choose from these chapters in any order you wish and according to your child or student's needs. Chances are, slightly older kids will find certain chapters more relevant, while slightly younger kids will prefer other chapters. You know your child best, so you get to choose when and how to use each of the chapters.

We applaud you for wanting to safeguard your children. The fact that you're holding this book is a good sign of things to come. These conversations might seem daunting to you, but you can do it! We have complete confidence in you and your kids. Because of parents and teachers like you, it really is possible to stand up to sexting!

With admiration,

Christy Monson and Heather Boynton

PART I

THINGS YOU NEED TO KNOW ABOUT SEXTING

FORWARD

TEXT

sexting:

Sending, forwarding, or receiving a
sexually explicit text message or image.

SHARE

POST

CHAPTER 1

WHAT IS SEXTING?

LEARN

Adolescence: Your Adventure of a Lifetime!

The older you get, the more you naturally want to figure out who you are. What makes you tick? What are you passionate about? What drives you nuts? Who do you like to spend time with? What

SNAP!

kind of person do you want to become? It's an exciting time of your life—perhaps the moment when you
feel like life is finally beginning!

Of course, the more you learn about yourself,
the more you'll want to tell the world: "THIS is ME!"
There are oodles of ways to do that—some healthy,
some not so much—and because of the exciting age
you're growing up in, one of your most common tools
will probably be technology. You might post pictures,
update your relationship status on social media, or
talk about your life (or breakfast . . . or dog . . . or
breakfast that tasted like dog).

And almost certainly, you'll find yourself sending and receiving text messages. Texting is amazing! It allows you to express yourself social-ly in so many ways (just look at all those emojis!). But some teens will take texting even further and turn it into *sexting*. That's when someone sends, receives, or forwards sexually explicit images. These sext messag-es might be of oneself or of someone else, but they always include nude or partially nude images and might also be referred to as "nudes."

"nude":

A common nickname for an image of naked or partially naked people.

It might seem like sexting is a great way to express yourself and explore your body, but in reality, it's one of the most dangerous things you can do. We'll explore why in later chapters, but for now, can you spot the difference between a text message and a sext message?

STORY

Aim for the Moon?

Alisha and her friends sent dozens of pictures to each other everyday. They took pictures of their pets, food, funny things they saw at school, and endless selfies. They were always competing to see who could send the funniest picture. Two of Alisha's friends were on the football team and loved taking pictures of themselves while working out, shirts off, pretending to be bodybuilders. One day in the locker room, two of the friends, Logan and Kai, were showering after a long, hot practice. Logan was first in the shower and was out quickly. Kai had stayed back to help put away the football gear and was the last one in the shower. Logan thought a quick picture of Kai's backside would be the perfect backdrop for a funny meme. Logan snapped the picture and added the words, "Aim for the Moon!" and he sent it to Alisha and their close friend group. Logan was sure this would qualify as the funniest picture yet!

CONVERSATION

Let's Talk About It!

? What types of pictures or messages from the story would be considered a text?

? What types of pictures or messages would be considered a sext?

? Can you find examples of each in the story?

? Have you ever seen a sext message before? How did that make you feel?

In your own words, how would you describe the difference between a text and a sext?

_____

_____

_____

_____

_____

_____

_____

_____

_____

_____

_____

_____

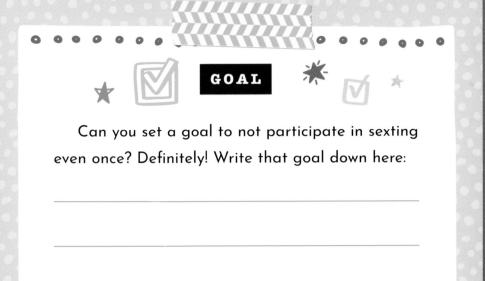

GOAL

Can you set a goal to not participate in sexting even once? Definitely! Write that goal down here:

_____

_____

_____

_____

_____

_____

_____

_____

_____

_____

_____

_____

CHAPTER 2

Sexting and Your Brain

LEARN

A Brief Tour of Your Brain

To understand why sexting is so dangerous, we'll first have to take a quick field trip to your brain (and remember, keep your hands and feet inside the cranium at all times). There are parts in your brain for making decisions, storing memory, and even running from danger. And amid all of that is a special part you might not have thought about before: your reward center. This part tells you when something is pleasurable by releasing a chemical called dopamine into your brain. Here's the trick though: your brain can't tell the difference between pleasures. Whether

neurotransmitter:

Chemicals in your brain that help neurons (communication cells in your nervous system) send messages to each other.

dopamine:

A type of neurotransmitter that sends signals to your nerve cells. One of its roles in telling your brain that something is pleasurable.

that comes from a tasty food, a good workout, or a drug, the brain registers it all the same: pleasure.

The problem is that when you view something sexual, like a sext message, dopamine is released and the brain's reward system becomes completely flooded. The more dopamine you have in your brain, the more you'll want to repeat the behavior that led to that pleasurable feeling. This is how addictions form.

★ **STORY**

Double Dopamine

Jonah loved pizza. Like, 'til death do us part kind of love. Cheese or pepperoni, cold for breakfast or warm straight out of the box, he loved it. And so it was no surprise to his friends what Jonah picked for lunch that day. It was warm, cheesy, gooey, just out of the oven with a little steam rising from the top in that way that lets you know this will be the best pizza you've ever tasted. He ate his two slices and then . . . *ahhhhhhhh*. His stomach full, Jonah spent the rest of his lunch period happily joking with his friends about Mr. Thornton's newest hairstyle—they were *sure* it was a toupee.

When school let out, Jonah waited for his ride like usual on the steps in front of the school. He

Remember: your brain can't tell the difference between pleasures. Whether that comes from a tasty food, a good workout, or a drug, the brain registers it all the same: pleasure.

pulled out his phone to check his text messages and saw that his friend Brad had sent him a photo. But it wasn't the usual—it was a woman in a swimsuit. Though Jonah felt it was probably inappropriate, he couldn't help sort of liking what he saw. He felt good in a way, like he'd just eaten his favorite pizza—but he wasn't full. He wanted to feel it again. He started a Google search for some more pictures like he'd seen, but then he stopped himself. "What's going on with me?" he thought.

CONVERSATION

Let's Talk About It!

? How did the pizza make Jonah feel? How did the sext message from Brad make Jonah feel? Why was it similar?

? Why didn't Jonah want to keep eating more pizza? But why did he want to see more pictures?

? What could have happened if Jonah had decided to keep going on with his Google search?

? Given what you've learned, what would you do if you were Jonah and you got the sext message from Brad?

JOURNAL

What have you learned about dopamine? Can you think of healthy times your brain has given you a good feeling?

_____

_____

_____

_____

_____

_____

_____

_____

_____

_____

_____

_____

_____

_____

_____

_____

GOAL

At some point in your life, you're probably going to be exposed to an inappropriate image. Can you set a goal right now for what you'll do if that happens? How will you respond? Who will you tell?

_____

_____

_____

_____

_____

Unlike footprints in the sand, the digital messages you send to others are never really gone. We call this a *digital footprint*.

CHAPTER 3

Your Digital Footprints

LEARN

Going, Going, Gone . . . Or Is It?

Have you ever gone for a walk on the beach and felt your feet sink into the wet sand? Your footprint leaves a trail showing your exact path of travel. Sometimes you can see where other people or animals, like birds, dogs, or horses, have traveled as well. But what happens when a wave comes up and washes over that footprint? Yes! It disappears. The wave acts like a giant eraser, and you can no longer see your tracks.

Unlike a sandy footprint that can be washed away by a wave, once digital data has been shared online, it is impossible to ever fully remove it from the Internet.

Unlike footprints in the sand, however, the digital messages you send to others are never really gone. We call this a *digital footprint*. These are the tracks you create while using the Internet. Your tracks can be formed by the text messages you send, the websites you visit, the information you send through social media, and the things you search for. The most important thing to remember is to be **wise** about your footprint and the tracks you leave behind. Unlike a sandy footprint that has been washed away by a wave, once digital data has been shared online, it is impossible to ever fully remove it from the Internet.

STORY

Vanishing Trick

In Luis's second-period leadership class, students were asked to compile pictures from the school year to create an end-of-the-year slideshow. As the students talked and shared their pictures, several were busy talking about the new social media app that promised to delete pictures just moments after they posted. While the teacher was busy writing on the board, several of the students sent messages to each other, testing out the new app. Luis sent a selfie to Abby across the room. Carson sent him a picture of Carlos breakdancing at the school dance, and in seconds, the picture was gone. Luis was amazed! He tried to look for the picture, but it seemed to have disappeared.

At lunch, Luis and several kids from his leadership class thought they'd try something a little more daring. Devin, Luis's best friend, had recently been sent a sext from a girl in his English class in hopes of starting a relationship. Devin quickly posted the

picture to the guys in the group, and again, within seconds, the picture seemed to vanish. The boys laughed in disbelief when they saw the picture, but Luis took a screenshot and saved it to his phone before the picture disappeared.

The next day in leadership, each student met with the teacher to share their photo contributions for the slideshow. Luis sat by his teacher, pulled up his photo album, and scrolled through his photos. As he swiped his finger to the right, the nude picture Devin had posted was exposed. Luis and Devin were horrified. Devin didn't realize anyone had saved the picture. Luis's teacher took Luis's phone and walked him and Devin to the main office. Luis, Devin, and the girl in the photo were all expelled and local authorities were called in to review the content.

CONVERSATION

Let's Talk About It!

? What is a digital footprint and how do you make one?

? Can pictures and messages you send ever fully be removed from the Internet? What about apps that promise to erase them?

? What could Devin and Luis have done to avoid this situation? What about the girl in the photo?

JOURNAL

Even though digital footprints seem to be gone, they never really are. What are some possible ways your footprint will stay around?

_____

_____

_____

_____

How would you feel knowing that you've spread inappropriate pictures in your footprints? How would you feel differently knowing you never did?

_____

_____

_____

_____

_____

_____

_____

_____

_____

GOAL

What goal will you set for yourself to make sure your digital footprints are always clean and wholesome?

_____

_____

_____

_____

_____

_____

PART II

WHAT IF SOMEONE WANTS ME TO PARTICIPATE IN SEXTING?

CHAPTER 4

AMONG FRIENDS

LEARN

Sexting Is No Joke, No Matter Who's Involved

Even if your pictures are innocent and seem just for fun (and let's be honest: are they *really*?), you have no control over what happens to them when they hit social media. What starts among friends can quickly end up in places and with people you never thought possible. What can you do to protect yourself, even among friends?

STORY

Stolen Moon

Jeremy and his older brother, Liam, were only a year apart. Sometimes people called them twins. They both played on the basketball team and were friends with most of the players. When Jeremy got home from practice, he mooned Liam before he

42

got in the shower. Liam snapped a photo of the moment and showed it to his brother. Both boys laughed.

The next day during basketball practice, Jeremy and Liam's friend, Sam, scrolled through Liam's photos. He found the picture of Jeremy's backside and sent it to a few more of their buddies. Everyone thought it was hilarious—except Liam and Jeremy. One of the other kids put kisses all over the picture and sent it to more guys—and even a few girls.

Jeremy and Liam were embarrassed and were angry with Sam.

"It was just for fun," Sam said. "I didn't put the kisses on it. Somebody else did that."

"That's not my idea of fun," Liam said.

CONVERSATION

Let's Talk About It!

? What could Liam have done differently?

? What should he do now?

? What could Jeremy have done differently?

? What should he do now?

? What about Sam? Were his actions okay? What should he do?

? If you were one of the boys who received the picture from Sam, what could you have done?

JOURNAL

Even our best friends can make mistakes and cause us harm. Can you think of a time that might have happened to you?

_____

_____

_____

_____

_____

What does this teach you about sharing something inappropriate, even with your friends?

_____

_____

_____

_____

_____

_____

_____

_____

_____

★ **GOAL**

What goal will you set for yourself to make sure you don't share anything inappropriate with your friends? And what about if they share something inappropriate with you?

_____

_____

_____

_____

_____

_____

Though it might seem like sexting can bring the two of you together, in the end, you'll end up just finding drama and sleepless nights.

CHAPTER 5

BOYFRIENDS AND GIRLFRIENDS

LEARN

Love ≠ Sexting

One of the most common places sexting happens is between boyfriends and girlfriends. You might think it will deepen your relationship if you share intimate pictures with each other. You may have even seen intimate pictures of your friends, so you want to do the same. The thing is, sexting actually does the opposite! It creates pressure, stress, and can reduce the trust and security in a relationship. Think of it this way: if you *really* love and care about someone, you wouldn't want to risk them getting in trouble with inappropriate pictures, would you?

Remember: you will date many people before you eventually marry, and that means that at some point, this relationship will end. What will you do then? Do you really want to have shared such personal photos with someone that you eventually will no longer be dating? And though your boyfriend or girlfriend promises to never share these images right now, will they always keep that promise after you break up?

It's important to keep in mind that you are just learning about friendship and love. During the next many years, you will try on lots of different relationships to find the best fit. You will need to spend time with many different people before you decide on a permanent relationship. That process will be much harder if sexting is involved and there is too much pressure for intimate romance.

So just remember: though it might seem like sexting can bring the two of you together, in the end, you're more likely to find drama and sleepless nights.

STORY

Friends Forever?

Shania and Markus had been good friends since grade school. When they got their phones, they Facetimed each other every night before bed. Markus loved talking with Shania, but he also wanted pictures he could keep. "So I can scroll through them before I fall asleep," he told Shania. As they talked, he took several screenshots every night.

Through junior high, they shared pictures on Snapchat each night before they went to bed. At first it was just sleepy poses with kissy lips. Then Shania sculpted

Though your boyfriend or girlfriend promises to never share these images right now, will they always keep that promise after you break up?

her hair on the pillow in a sexy way and sent the picture with a suggestive message. They both began sending more daring pictures, with Shania in a see-through nightie and Markus bare-chested.

One night, Shania called Markus crying. She was afraid her parents would find out about their pictures. "You worry too much," Markus pressured. "They go away after a few seconds." But he secretly kept screenshots of many of them.

As they entered high school, Shania and Markus met new friends. Shania still liked Markus, but she wanted to meet new guys. There were some cute ones in her geometry class. She wanted to get to know them, and she began to see other guys behind Markus's back.

Markus was hurt and angry when he found out. He felt betrayed and wanted to get back at Shania. He plastered the screenshots he'd saved of Shania's bedtime photos all over social media. One of the boys took the pictures to the school counselor. The police were called in.

CONVERSATION

Let's Talk About It!

? What could Shania have done differently?

? What could Markus have done differently?

? How did sexting affect their relationship?

JOURNAL

Sexting can cause a lot of stress in a relationship. Why do you think that is?

GOAL

What can you do to make sure your relationships are healthy and wholesome?

You should always seek help when you get included in something that you feel is wrong. Not only could you help protect a victim, but you'll also be protecting yourself.

CHAPTER 6

WHAT ABOUT BYSTANDERS?

LEARN

Bystanders Have a Responsibility

Sometimes, you might find yourself in a situation where you aren't involved in sexting directly but as a bystander. It could be a group text where someone shares a picture of a kid at school, or maybe a social media post you happen to see in your feed. You didn't ask for it—you didn't even want it—but there it is. What should you do? Do you even *have* to do anything? **Absolutely.** You should always seek help when you get included in something that you feel is wrong. Not only could you help protect a victim, but you'll also be protecting yourself.

bystander:
A person who is present but who doesn't participate.

STORY

Guilty by Association

Vanessa was invited to a summer swim party with the popular kids. She'd never been asked before and was excited to go.

"There'll be alcohol," her older brother, Ben, said. "I went to a party there once. I left when everyone got drunk and didn't go again."

"Not a problem for me," Vanessa said. "I'm not going to drink."

She went shopping for a cute new swimsuit.

At the party, some of the girls' outfits were so revealing that Vanessa feel uncomfortable. Some of the boys snapped pictures and took sexy videos. Vanessa stayed in the background, feeling trapped. She changed back into her normal clothes—she didn't like the look of those videos. Oh, how she wanted to leave! But she couldn't think of an excuse.

Vanessa took a sip of punch. It was spiked, so she set the glass back on the table. Several boys bypassed the punch and pulled out their own brown bags.

The drunker and louder everyone got, the more uncomfortable Vanessa felt.

Boys and girls began posting pictures on Instagram and Snapchat. Even though she didn't want to, they pulled Vanessa into some of the photos.

By midnight, Vanessa finally slipped away from the party without saying anything to anyone.

The next day, she heard that some parents had called the police. An investigation was underway, accusing the party-goers of posting underage pornography.

Vanessa felt scared. She was in some of the pictures.

CONVERSATION

Let's Talk About It!

? What could Vanessa have done differently?

? What should she do now?

? What could Ben have done differently?

? What should he do now?

POWERFUL BYSTANDERS

Research says that when a bystander who witnesses bullying decides to intervene, the bullying stops within ten seconds nearly sixty percent of the time.[6] You have more power than you think! So here are ways you can help:

- Let an adult know what's happening.
- Say you're not interested in mean gossip.
- Decide not to listen to the rude comments on the bully's social media.
- Be friends with the person hurt by the bullying and let him or her know you care.
- Tell the bully to stop.

There are many reasons a bystander might fear getting involved. What do you think some of them are?

_____

_____

_____

_____

_____

Think about Vanessa at the party. Even if you don't do anything wrong yourself, you can still get in trouble for being involved. Why do you think that is?

_____

_____

_____

_____

_____

_____

_____

_____

_____

_____

GOAL

What can you decide to do to prevent yourself or others from being part of an inappropriate situation? Who will you ask for help? Decide now and write their names.

_____

_____

_____

_____

_____

PART III

HOW TO AVOID BEING A SEXTING VICTIM

NETIQUETTE

Netiquette is one of the simplest
and most powerful ways to avoid
a sexting trap.

CHAPTER 7

THE POWER OF NETIQUETTE

LEARN

The Golden Rule Works

When using the Internet, texting, or browsing social media, you should always treat others the way you would like to be treated and try to help them do the same. We'll call this *netiquette*. Fortunately, netiquette is easy to do. And even better, netiquette is one of the most powerful ways to avoid

a sexting trap. Read the following story and see if you can identify how netiquette could have changed the outcome.

STORY

Caught in a Trap!

"Class," Ms. C. said, "the subject today is netiquette. Define *netiquette*."

Iringa raised her hand. "Internet etiquette."

"Okay." Ms. C. pushed her glasses up on her nose. "What does netiquette mean to you?"

Patty raised her eyebrows. "Don't scam your friends online."

"Or your enemies," Marcherelle chuckled.

"Be nice to others, and they will be nice to you—maybe," Garth said.

"Great ideas—all good points." Ms. C rubbed her hands together.

"Here's a story I heard from a parent the other day," the teacher continued. "A girl—let's use the name Molly—went shopping for a new swimsuit, and she found a classy bikini. When she was in the dressing room trying it on, she took a selfie and texted it to her best friend, Beth, to show her how cute it was and how well it fit."

David let out a cat-call. Everyone laughed.

Ms. C. frowned at David and continued. "Innocent, right?"

Everyone nodded.

"Later that day, Beth and her older brother got into a fight. He was so mad at Beth that he grabbed her phone and locked himself in the bathroom. While she banged on the door, he swiped through her texts and found Molly's swimsuit picture. He sent it to himself and then blasted it to all his friends. Molly was devastated. She felt exposed and betrayed."

CONVERSATION

Let's Talk About It!

? What could Molly have done differently?

? What should she do now?

? What could Beth have done differently?

? What should she do now?

? What could Older Brother have done differently?

? What should he do now?

? Look at the Netiquette Rules below. If each person in this story had followed the rules, how would the outcome have been different?

? If you were the parent of one of these kids, what would you do?

NETIQUETTE RULES

- Be kind.
- Respect others' privacy.
- Don't forward information that's not about you.
- Use clean language.
- Send your feelings with emojis, not with all caps, which is like yelling.
- Did I say, be kind?

JOURNAL

How can following netiquette rules protect you and others from a sexting trap?

_____

_____

_____

_____

_____

GOAL

Are there any netiquette rules you could do better at? Make a goal to improve!

_____

_____

_____

_____

Bullies usually stay clear of kids who are involved in the positive activities of a busy student. Good self-esteem is the best bully protection you can have!

CHAPTER 8

DEALING WITH SEXTING CYBERBULLIES

LEARN

The Best Form of Protection

Sometimes, no matter how hard you try to do the right thing, there are other people who seem determined to make things hard for you. It would be great if we could put on a bully-protection shield to keep us from being exposed to bullying or sexting.

BULLY PROTECTION

Here are some ideas to help you become your best self:

- Join school clubs or other after-school activities and sports.
- Enjoy activities with friends that don't involve electronics.
- Spend time working and playing with your family.
- Join a community or church youth group and serve others.
- Be a good student.
- Develop your talents, such as sports, music, or art.
- Every night before bed, think of three good things you did that day.

But, since that isn't possible, the next best thing is to focus on becoming the very best person we can be. Bullies usually stay clear of kids who are involved in the positive activities of a busy student. Good self-esteem is the best bully protection you can have.

STORY

Groveling for Money

Larisa loved to be involved in school activities. She was busy with dancing and soccer. She had friends in those activities, but her best friend was Tonya, first-chair flute player in the band. They both belonged to the school service club.

Larisa and Tonya had just collected pennies for the children's hospital from the lunch crowd and were taking them back to their advisor's room. Someone knocked the bag out of Larisa's hands and pennies and other loose change cascaded all over the floor. Larisa and Tonya bent over to pick up all the money, and a student took embarrassing pictures of Larisa's backside while she was on the ground. That afternoon, most of the kids in school received it with the caption: "Groveling for money."

Larisa and Tonya just smiled and texted a picture of the recollected bag of money with the caption: "Bending our backs for the children's hospital."

Everyone laughed and the incident was forgotten.

CONVERSATION

Let's Talk About It!

? How would you have felt if a picture like that of you was sent to everyone in the school?

? What did Larisa do right?

? What kind of a friend was Tonya?

? Why were Larisa and Tonya able to handle the bully's effort to upset them?

CYBERBULLY CURE

Research says that only twenty to thirty percent of kids who have been bullied tell an adult.[7] Be one of those kids. You'll feel so much better if you don't keep the secret. Secrets carry emotional power. Don't give the bully that power. Take it back for yourself.

- If you get an embarrassing or sexting message, don't respond immediately.
- Take a time-out and cool off.
- Show your parents, a teacher, or a trusted friend.
- With the help of an adult, go to the police if necessary.
- Talk with other kids you trust about the problem.
- Listen to their experiences. You'll both feel better.

CHOOSE YOUR FRIENDS CAREFULLY

One of the things Larisa and Tonya did right was choose friends who could be trusted. They both knew they could count on each other.

Here's a helpful idea about friendship: keep people close or distant according to how safe they are to talk to and to share feelings with:

- There are some kids who send hurtful text messages. Put these kids in the outside circle. You should still be kind to them, but don't share personal things with them. When these kids say mean things about others, you know that one day they might do the same to you.
- Put your acquaintances in the middle circle. They are kids you study with at school or who belong to the same clubs or activities. They are nice, but you don't know them well enough to share your inner feelings.
- Put your close friends in the inner circle. They can be trusted! They won't betray you.

There's space on the next page to try it out!

One more important thought: Could you be a sexting cyberbully? We've all done things we're not proud of. In today's world, that can include the misuse of electronics and the Internet. Have you been part of a cyberbully or sexting plot? What do you need to change?

 JOURNAL

Create your own circles of friendship below. Who's in the inner circle? Who's in the middle circle? And who's in the outer circle?

What else have you learned about the power of friendship and self-esteem?

_____

_____

_____

_____

_____

GOAL

Is there a goal you might want to set to help you develop good self-esteem and healthy friendships?

_____

_____

_____

_____

CHAPTER 9

STAYING SAFE FROM PREDATORS

LEARN

Cyber Strangers

You would never pass out cards with your address and phone number to strangers you met on the street, would you? It's the same with the Internet. Keep yourself and your information safe by not sharing it with others, even if it seems okay to do so. Not everyone on the Internet are as they seem.

STORY

Underage

Yolanda loved her new smartphone. She was only twelve when her mother got it for her, and Yolanda promised, even though she was young, that she would keep herself safe. Her mother was relieved that Yolanda had a phone because she could keep in touch with her throughout the day. But still, she worried.

Yolanda put her phone charger right on the bookcase next to her special American Girl doll collection so she could plug her phone in each night before she went to bed.

Yolanda knew that thirteen was the minimum age for Facebook, Instagram, and Snapchat accounts. She would be thirteen in a little over eight months. What would it hurt for her to create a false account? It was easy, so she joined. She felt very grown-up as she began chatting with newfound social media friends.

Online she met a girl, Tammy, about her age. They became fast friends. They both loved American Girl dolls. Tammy had a doll that Yolanda really wanted to see: Molly, the World War II doll. They decided to meet at a local park. Yolanda was so excited to see Tammy's doll.

Yolanda texted her mother that she'd be late coming home from school because she was going to the park with a friend. As she walked from school to the park, her mother drove by and rolled down the car window.

"What are you doing here?" Yolanda asked.

"I forgot you had a dental appointment to get your braces tightened this afternoon."

Yolanda climbed in the car and slammed the door. "I wanted to hang out with my new friend, Tammy. She has Molly, the World War II doll. That's a rare doll, and I wanted to see her." Mom touched her shoulder. "I'm sorry. Let's circle the park and tell Tammy I forgot your dental appointment. You can set another day to meet."

predator:

A person or an animal that hunts a smaller weaker person or animal. Often, as in this case, for sexual purposes.

Mom slowed as she neared the park. There was a middle-aged man waiting on the corner where Yolanda was to meet Tammy. He was holding an American Girl doll—Molly. Yolanda clenched her arms to her chest. Mother grabbed Yolanda's arm and held on. Both were shocked.

CONVERSATION

Let's Talk About It!

? Was there any danger in this situation?

? What had happened? What *could* have happened?

? What could Yolanda have done differently?

? What should she do now?

? What could Mom have done differently?

? What should she do now?

This is a situation where the police needed to be involved. Many times, predators pose as young people and trick them into sending pornographic images. Luckily, that didn't happen to Yolanda. It's very possible this man may have abused many victims before her and would abuse many after her if he was not caught.

KID SAFETY RULES

- Don't join social media until you are old enough! And even then, decide with your parents first what age is best for you. Just because you can legally join a site doesn't mean it's the right time for you.
- Don't give out personal information without your parents' permission, including your last name, home address, telephone number, and the name of your school.
- Create a screen name that does not contain any of your personal information like your name or birth date.
- Never share your password with anyone but your parents.
- Don't post photos or videos of yourself or anyone else without your parents' consent.
- Don't get together with an online friend unless your parents agree to it.
- If you receive any messages that are unkind, talk to your parents or a teacher immediately.
- Don't create fake profiles to be cool.

JOURNAL

Can you always tell if someone is a predator online? Why not?

_____

_____

_____

_____

_____

GOAL

Look at the list of kid safety rules. Are there some you could follow better? Make a goal!

_____

_____

_____

_____

PART IV

OTHER IMPORTANT CONVERSATIONS

CHAPTER 10

WHAT IF I MAKE A MISTAKE?

LEARN

Mistakes Might Happen, But You Can Overcome Them

Sometimes we make mistakes. It's human, and it happens to all of us: your parents, your teachers, everyone. It can be tough to fess up to a mistake. You might feel embarrassed. You might worry what your parents will think or what your friends will say. The consequences might loom so large that you wonder if you'll ever recover. The world could feel like it's ending.

The thing is, mistakes, like secrets, always grow over time. The more you hold something in, the larger and heavier it will be to carry. No matter what mistake happened, you will feel so much better if you talk to a trusted adult about it. Plus, they'll be able to help you figure out a solution to anything that might have happened. **You never have to handle something alone.**

STORY

Blackmailed

Remi was one of the most popular kids in school. He was in the National Honor Society, started for the varsity football team, and was friends with just about everyone on social media. To top it all, he'd just won a prestigious scholarship to his dream college. Everything was going right.

One night, Remi was lying in bed scrolling through his newest text messages. He was just about to go to sleep when he saw a message from a number he didn't recognize. He opened it, and it was from a girl named Gabriela. He'd never met her before and knew better than to talk with a stranger, but she seemed so nice. Soon, Remi and Gabriela were texting back and forth and sharing everything together.

But Gabriela said she wanted Remi to share more. In fact, she sent him a racy picture of herself—and pressured him to send her one back. Remi hesitated, but he gave in. He felt a little embarrassed, but he sent her the nude photo of himself anyway.

A few minutes later, Gabriela texted back: "Thanks for the photo. Send me $500, or I'm going to send it to all of your friends on Facebook."

Remi's stomach was in knots. He'd fallen for a trap. He stayed awake all night not knowing what to do, and in the morning, Gabriela texted again: "I mean it. Pay me now or I'm sharing."

This was getting serious. He could pay her the money, but he knew she'd just ask for more. But what if she posted the photo? Remi could lose everything that mattered to him. What would his parents say? Would he lose his scholarship? Would he get in trouble with the police? The more his mind raced, the more he felt trapped in a deep, dark hole.

Over the next several days, Remi's despair got worse and worse—and so did Gabriela's demands. Finally, Remi decided he had to talk to someone.

After school, he asked his parents if they could chat for a few minutes with him. He told them what had happened, and to his surprise, his mom and dad were more concerned for him than they were upset. His mom called an attorney who helped them walk through the steps of handling a blackmailer. His dad helped him lock down his social media accounts' friend lists so Gabriela couldn't send anything to them. They documented everything and got in touch with authorities who later tracked down the blackmailer. It turned out that "Gabriela" was actually a fifty-year-old man in Texas who was extorting dozens of people for money!

It wasn't easy going through all of that, but eventually Remi was free. He felt so relieved. And most of all, he loved his parents even more after seeing all the support they gave him through one of his darkest moments.

CONVERSATION

Let's Talk About It!

? Are you surprised by how Remi's parents reacted? Why or why not?

? What do you think would have happened if Remi hadn't talked with someone about his situation?

? Have you ever felt alone with a problem? What does Remi's story teach you?

THERE IS ALWAYS HOPE

Remember: The sun does rise again! Don't ever despair, no matter how serious a mistake seems to you. With help from trusted adults, you can get through anything.

Imagine you were a parent. What would you say to your child if he or she came to you with a problem like Remi's?

_____

_____

_____

_____

_____

_____

_____

_____

_____

_____

What does that teach you about how most grownups would respond to you, too?

_____

_____

_____

_____

_____

★ ☑ **GOAL** ✳ ☑ ★

What trusted adults do you know who you could talk to about a mistake you made? Make a list of those people, then promise yourself that you won't handle future problems on your own!

_____

_____

_____

_____

_____

CHAPTER 11

But I Reeaaally Want a Smartphone!

25%

100%

LEARN

What's Your Trust Level?

When it seems all your friends at school have smartphones, you might think you'll burst if you don't have one, too! There are many good ways a phone can help you with communication and safety. But there are also many distracting—even harmful—things a phone can do. Your parents know you best, and they will decide when the right age is for you. Having a smartphone is a big responsibility that requires a lot of trust, so the best thing you can do now is show your parents that you are worthy of that trust. Then, when the time is right, your parents will know they can trust you to make wise decisions with your new device.

Read the story below and consider this: are you flaky like Jake, or are you trustworthy?

STORY

Flaky Jake

Jake, age thirteen, *really* wanted a new smartphone. He begged his parents. "All the kids have one. What about me?"

"We'll see," his dad said. "They cost a lot of money."

"Show us you'll be responsible," his mom said. "Dad and I will talk about it."

Jake was supposed to clean his room on Saturday, but his friends got a pick-up basketball game going at the school, and he decided to join them. He was too tired that night after playing basketball to make

his bed and put away his clothes. Then the next day, Samantha called and asked him to go to the movies. They went for pizza after, and it was too late again when he got home. He'd clean his room next weekend.

His social studies teacher had a pop quiz on Monday. Jake hadn't read the material. He got a D on the test. It was also his turn to give a report in Spanish class, but he forgot. The teacher told him he could give it the next day. He scrambled to put something together, but it was last minute and he only got a C on it.

"Please, Dad," Jake said. "I really want a smartphone."

"Did you get your chores done this weekend?" Mom asked. "And how is school going?"

"Well, uh . . ." Jake didn't know what to say.

CONVERSATION

Let's Talk About It!

? Would you give Jake a new smartphone? Why or why not?

? How do we build trust?

BUILDING TRUST

There are many ways you can build trust with your parents and family. Here are a few ideas. What more could you add to the list?

- Follow family rules.
- Complete household and school work.
- Be honest in your relationships with others.

RESPONSIBILITIES AND PRIVILEGES

You should have as many responsibilities in helping with family duties as you have privileges. The more you are willing to help and keep your word, the more your parents will be willing to trust you. Jake wasn't trustworthy, so his parents were hesitant about giving him extra privileges.

Here's a possible list of responsibilities and privileges.

Responsibilities

- Let your parents know where you are.
- Keep your room clean.
- Do your homework.

Privileges

- Spend time with friends.
- Have friends over.
- Join a sports team.

This is just a sample. Create your own list with your parents on the next page to see where you stand. With this list, you and your parents will know how responsible you are. The more trustworthy you are, the more privileges you can have. Be reliable so they can count on you. Show them you can be trusted.

JOURNAL

Make a list of your responsibilities:

RESPONSIBILITIES

_____

_____

_____

_____

_____

_____

_____

_____

_____

_____

_____

Now make a list of your privileges:

PRIVILEGES

_____

_____

_____

_____

_____

_____

_____

_____

_____

_____

Review your lists. How responsible do you think you are? Are you making it possible to have privileges? What do your parents say?

_____

_____

_____

_____

_____

_____

_____

_____

_____

_____

_____

GOAL

What changes do you plan to make to increase your trust level?

_____

_____

_____

_____

_____

_____

_____

_____

_____

_____

CHAPTER 12

Using the Internet for Good

LEARN

A Tool for Goodness

There is so much good on the Internet. Knowledge of the world is just a click away. Let's look at some of the ways the Internet can be used to help us become the best we can be.

STORY

Spreading Sunshine

Gordon watched the news one evening with his parents and was discouraged at all the negative things he saw happening in the world. That night, he couldn't sleep. The more he thought about it, the more discouraged he felt. What could anyone do when things seemed so bleak? But slowly, his mind came around to an idea: if he couldn't change the world, he could at least change *his* world.

Gordon decided to counter what he'd seen by spreading positivity among his friends and family. Each day, he sent them a happy message. Sometimes he sent a "Hi" with balloons. Sometimes fireworks. Maybe an emoji with a "Hey Buddy" or a "Hello Sunshine."

It didn't take long before his messaging caught on and kids texted him back. He received friendly notes every day. He and his buddies shared their positive emojis with other kids in the school, and soon, his circle of friends expanded to all those who wanted to participate. Gordon couldn't believe how his world had turned around.

CONVERSATION

Let's Talk About It!

? Do you like Gordon's idea?

? Have you ever received a positive text like Gordon's? How did it make you feel? If not, what would it mean to you to receive one from some-one?

SPREAD MORE SUNSHINE

There are many more ideas for using the Internet for good. Here are a few that people have actually done! What can you add to this list?

- Gather donations to feed the homeless.
- Pay the tuition for kids from low-income families so they can play sports.
- Raise funds to build homes for disabled kids in Africa.
- Throw birthday parties for kids who've never had a party.
- Raise awareness for endangered animals.
- Connect with family who live far away.
- Host a spontaneous party.
- Start a kindness campaign.

You can find happiness in your cyberspace! Just remember that the best happiness will come from a life balanced with online and offline activities.

JOURNAL

There are many things in life that can be used for both good and bad. Can you think of other examples?

_____

_____

_____

_____

In the story about Gordon, just one person was able to start an entire movement. How did that happen?

_____

_____

_____

_____

GOAL

Make a list of people that you'd like to send positive text messages to:

_____

_____

_____

_____

_____

_____

_____

_____

Plan what you'll say in your texts and make a goal to send the messages.

Now, brainstorm some other ways you can use your phone or the Internet to do good:

_____

_____

_____

_____

_____

_____

_____

_____

_____

_____

Pick one and make a goal to do it!

NOTES

1   "Top 10 Child Health Problems: More Concern for Sexting, Internet Safety."
    National Poll on Children's Health. https://mottpoll.org/reports-surveys/top-
    10-child-health-problems-more-concern-sexting-internet-safety.

2   Gassó, Klettke, Agustina, and Montiel. "Sexting, Mental Health, and
    Victimization Among Adolescents: A Literature Review." *International
    Journal of Environmental Research and Public Health* 16, no. 13 (March
    2019): 2364. https://doi.org/10.3390/ijerph16132364.

3   Galovan, Adam M., Michelle Drouin, and Brandon T. Mcdaniel. "Sexting
    Profiles in the United States and Canada: Implications for Individual and
    Relationship Well-Being." *Computers in Human Behavior* 79 (2018): 19-29.
    https://doi.org/10.1016/j.chb.2017.10.017.

4   Hilton, Donald L. "Pornography Addiction - a Supranormal Stimulus
    Considered in the Context of Neuroplasticity." *Socioaffective Neuroscience
    & Psychology* 3, no. 1 (2013): 20767. https://doi.org/10.3402/snp.v3i0.20767.

5   Madigan, Sheri, Anh Ly, Christina L. Rash, Joris Van Ouytsel, and Jeff R.
    Temple. "Prevalence of Multiple Forms of Sexting Behavior Among Youth."
    JAMA Pediatrics 172, no. 4 (January 2018): 327. https://doi.org/10.1001/
    jamapediatrics.2017.5314.

6   Hawkins, D. Lynn, Debra J. Pepler, and Wendy M. Craig. "Naturalistic
    Observations of Peer Interventions in Bullying." *Social Development* 10, no. 4
    (2001): 512-27. https://doi.org/10.1111/1467-9507.00178.

7   Ttofi, Maria M., and David P. Farrington. "Effectiveness of School-Based
    Programs to Reduce Bullying: a Systematic and Meta-Analytic Review."
    Journal of Experimental Criminology 7, no. 1 (2010): 27-56. https://doi.
    org/10.1007/s11292-010-9109-1.

SOURCES

"5 Internet Safety Tips for Tweens and Teens." Scholastic. https://www.scholastic.com/parents/family-life/social-emotional-learning/technology-and-kids/5-internet-safety-tips-tweens-and-teens.html.

"Cyberbullying: The Role of Witnesses." MediaSmarts, November 20, 2015. http://mediasmarts.ca/digital-media-literacy/digital-issues/cyberbulling/cyberbullying-role-witnesses.

Educatorstechnology. "15 Essential Netiquette Guidelines to Share with Your Students." Educational Technology and Mobile Learning, June 11, 2014. https://www.educatorstechnology.com/2014/06/15-essential-netiquette-guidelines-to.html.

Friedman, Lindsay. "Parents Divided on Monitoring Their Kids' Internet Use." *USA Today*. Gannett Satellite Information Network, June 19, 2013. https://www.usatoday.com/story/news/nation/2013/06/19/kids-safety-online/2434513/.

Galovan, Adam M., Michelle Drouin, and Brandon T. Mcdaniel. "Sexting Profiles in the United States and Canada: Implications for Individual and Relationship Well-Being." *Computers in Human Behavior* 79 (2018): 19-29. https://doi.org/10.1016/j.chb.2017.10.017.

Gardiner, Steve. "Column: Students Are Addicted to Their Cellphones, and They Need Our Help." PBS. Public Broadcasting Service, May 13, 2016. https://www.pbs.org/newshour/education/column-students-are-addicted-to-their-cellphones-and-they-need-our-help.

Gassó, Klettke, Agustina, and Montiel. "Sexting, Mental Health, and Victimization Among Adolescents: A Literature Review." *International Journal of Environmental Research and Public Health* 16, no. 13 (March 2019): 2364. https://doi.org/10.3390/ijerph16132364.

Harris, Andrew & Davidson, Judith & Letourneau, Elizabeth & Paternite, Carl & Tusinski, Karin. (2013). "Building a Prevention Framework to Address Teen 'Sexting' Behaviors."

Hawkins, D. Lynn, Debra J. Pepler, and Wendy M. Craig. "Naturalistic Observations of Peer Interventions in Bullying." *Social Development* 10, no. 4 (2001): 512-27. https://doi.org/10.1111/1467-9507.00178.

Hilton, Donald L. "Pornography Addiction - a Supranormal Stimulus Considered in the Context of Neuroplasticity." *Socioaffective Neuroscience & Psychology* 3, no. 1 (2013): 20767. https://doi.org/10.3402/snp.v3i0.20767.

"Internet Safety Tips for Children and Teens." The New York Public Library. https://www.nypl.org/help/about-nypl/legal-notices/internet-safety-tips.

Isokpan, Esosa, Esosa Isokpan, Emma, Emma, An Anonymous Person, Areangeli, Areangeli, et al. "Cyberbullying Facts." Cyberbullying Research Center. https://cyberbullying.org/facts.

Jolly, Jennifer. "In 'Screenagers,' What to Do About Too Much Screen Time." *The New York Times*, March 15, 2016. https://well.blogs.nytimes.com/2016/03/15/in-screenagers-what-to-do-about-too-much-screen-time/.

"Keeping Kids Safe in Cyberspace:Teaching Internet Safety." The Center for Parenting Education. http://centerforparentingeducation.org/library-of-articles/kids-and-technology/keeping-kids-safe-in-cyberspace/.

Lim, M. S. C., Vella, A. M., Horyniak, D. R., & Hellard, M. E. (2016). "Exploring Attitudes Towards Sexting of Young People: A Cross-Sectional Study." *Sexual Health*, 13(6), 530. doi: 10.1071/sh16029.

Madigan, Sheri, Anh Ly, Christina L. Rash, Joris Van Ouytsel, and Jeff R. Temple. "Prevalence of Multiple Forms of Sexting Behavior Among Youth." *JAMA Pediatrics* 172, no. 4 (January 2018): 327. https://doi.org/10.1001/jamapediatrics.2017.5314.

"Netiquette." *Merriam-Webster*. https://www.merriam-webster.com/dictionary/netiquette.

"Netiquette Rules for Electronic Communications." Netiquette Rules. http://edtech2.boisestate.edu/frankm/573/netiquette.html.

NewsHour, PBS. "Your Phone Is Trying to Control Your Life." PBS. Public Broadcasting Service, January 31, 2017. https://www.pbs.org/newshour/show/phone-trying-control-life.

Ouytsel, J. V., Gool, E. V., Walrave, M., Ponnet, K., & Peeters, E. (2016). "Sexting: Adolescents' Perceptions of the Applications Used for, Motives for, and Consequences of Sexting." *Journal of Youth Studies*, 1-25. doi: 10.1080/13676261.2016.1241865.

"SafeKids.com." SafeKidscom. http://www.safekids.com/kids-rules-for-online-safety/.

"SafeKids.com." SafeKidscom. http://www.safekids.com/teen-pledge-for-being-smart-online/.

Social Media, and Madison Bell. "7 Teens Using Social Media for Good Deeds." Smart Social, October 15, 2019. https://smartsocial.com/teens-using-social-media-good-deeds/.

"Teens and Sexting: What Is It and What Can Parents Do?" (2012). *The Brown University Child and Adolescent Behavior Letter*, 28(S4). doi: 10.1002/cbl.20162

"Top 10 Child Health Problems: More Concern for Sexting, Internet Safety." National Poll on Children's Health. https://mottpoll.org/reports-surveys/top-10-child-health-problems-more-concern-sexting-internet-safety.

Ttofi, Maria M., and David P. Farrington. "Effectiveness of School-Based Programs to Reduce Bullying: a Systematic and Meta-Analytic Review." *Journal of Experimental Criminology* 7, no. 1 (2010): 27-56. https://doi.org/10.1007/s11292-010-9109-1.

Wagstaff, Keith. "Are Your Kids Addicted To Their Phones? 'Screenagers' Wants to Help." *Forbes*. February 29, 2016. https://www.forbes.com/sites/keithwagstaff/2016/02/28/are-your-kids-addicted-to-their-phones-screenagers-wants-to-help/#72e30a8763eb.

Walsh, D.. (2019). "Young People's Considerations and Attitudes Towards the Consequences of Sexting." *Educational and Child Psychology*. 36. 58-73.

Weisskirch, R. S., Drouin, M., & Delevi, R. (2016). "Relational Anxiety and Sexting." *The Journal of Sex Research*, 54(6), 685-693. doi: 10.1080/00224499.2016.1181147.

Further Reading

FOR YOUTH

Brown, Tracy. *Cyberbullying: Online Safety*. Rosen Publishing Group, New York, New York, 2014.

Jenson, Kristen A. *Good Pictures Bad Pictures: Porn-Proofing Today's Young Kids*. Glen Cove Press, Richland, Washington, 2018.

Raatma, Lucia. *Cyberbullying*. Children's Press, Scholastic, New York, New York, 2013.

Rowell, Rebecca. *Social Media: Like It or Leave It*. Compass Point Books, Capstone, North Mankato, Minnesota, 2015.

Runstedler, Nancy. *Pay It Forward Kids: Small Acts, Big Change*. Fitzhenry & Whiteside, Markham, Ontario, Canada, 2013.

Stuckey, Rachel. *Cyber Bullying: Take A Stand Against Bullying*. Crabtree Publishing, New York, New York, 2013.

Truesdell, Ann. *How to Handle Cyberbullies*. Cherry Lake Publishing, Ann Arbor, Michigan, 2014.

FOR ADULTS

Hitchcock, J.A. *Cyber Bullying and the Wild Wild Web*: What Everyone Needs to Know. Rowman and Littlefield Publishing Group, Lanham, Maryland, 2017.

McQuade, Samuel C., Sarah E. Gentry, Nathan W. Fisk. *Cybersafety, Cyberstalking & Cyberbullying*. Chelsea House, Infobase Learning Company, 2012.

Shariff, Shaheen. *Confronting Cyber-Bullying*. Cambridge University Press, New York, New York, 2009.

Trolley, Barbara C., Constance Hanel. *Cyber Kids, Cyber Bullying, Cyber Balance*. Corwin Publishing, Thousand Oaks, California. 2010.

About the Creators

CHRISTY MONSON

As a marriage and family therapist, Christy Monson spent years helping clients heal and reframe their lives in Las Vegas and Salt Lake City. She received her BA degree from Utah State University and her MS from University of Nevada at Las Vegas. The mother of six children and the grandmother of many grandchildren, Christy is now retired and lives in northern Utah. She is the author of several books, including *50 Real Heroes for Boys* (Bushel & Peck), *Love, Hugs, and Hope: When Scary Things Happen* (Familius), *Family Talk* (Familius), and *Becoming Free* (Familius).

HEATHER BOYNTON

Heather is a member of the Child Development Department at Clovis Community College. She received her MA in early childhood education from California State University. Before becoming a full-time professor, Heather worked as a preschool teacher and Programs for Infants and Toddlers (PITC) trainer. She was also a California Early Childhood Mentor Teacher. Heather lives in California with her husband, Dave, and their four kids.

ALBERT PINILLA

Albert Pinilla is a freelance illustrator based between Barcelona and Finland. He has worked for many publishers and companies including Editorial Casals, Editorial Sàpiens, Diset S.A, Goula, Editorial San Pablo, Descobrir, *Namaka* magazine, Editorial Mi Cuento, P/A/N, Capçalera, Davos Comunicación S.L, La Agencia de Publicidad S.A (Spain), Hannacroix Creek Books, Bookworks, *Highlights* magazine (U.S.), *Petit Dimoni* magazine (France), Headu Giochi (Italy), Igloo Books (United Kingdom), Schildts & Söderstrström s (Finland), and Akotek (Norway).

31192022030421